Contents

Introduction

China is a massive country. It has a population of almost 1.3 billion people, which is about one-fifth of all the people in the world. Over the last ten years, China's economy has been growing faster than any other nation's, at 10 per cent per year. However, it is still among the poorest countries in the world.

When pronouncing Chinese words it may be helpful to remember:
zh is said like j in jump
q is said like ch in chip
x is said like sh in shop

Since 1949, the communist party has ruled China. When the Communists came to power, they managed to raise the standard of living for most Chinese people. At the same time, however, many people were persecuted because of their beliefs. China closed its borders and isolated itself from the outside world.

Before the 1980s, everything was owned and controlled by the government. Then big changes took place: the rules were slowly relaxed, allowing people to run their own farms and businesses. The Chinese quickly took advantage of this. Now, thousands of people are running their own businesses in the hope of a better life.

China's cities are some of the most crowded in the world. In Shanghai, people throng the streets in one of the main shopping areas.

'I want an action-filled life, not a quiet life any more. If I have good fortune then I will make big money. If I don't, then at least I will die suddenly: I don't want to die gradually . . .'
– **Xie Zulian, self-employed tourist guide, South China**

Above Private traders make money selling souvenirs of Mao Zedong, China's former leader, to Western tourists.

Below One of China's most famous scenic areas, near Guilin. Fields of rice are grown in between the limestone peaks.

Where there had been empty shelves, shops are now full of goods. An 'open-door' policy has allowed foreigners in to do business, and the Chinese are learning about modern technology and skills.

However, problems lie in the path of smooth economic development. One is a lack of modern equipment and skills: most factories and farms still use primitive and labour-intensive methods. Transport and communications are poor and there is a shortage of power and skilled workers.

In this vast country, nuclear power and space programmes exist alongside simple farming techniques, and advanced cities contrast with backward country areas. In addition, the population is enormous and is still growing. Just to keep China's people fed, housed and clothed is a huge task, before sparing resources for modernization and development.

The land and its use

Because it is so far inland and receives little rain, the north-west of China is mostly desert.

China divides into two parts: the wild, unfarmed, western region and the farmed and settled east. Much of the western half consists of high, windswept mountains and plateau, lying at an average altitude of about 4,000 metres. Apart from grass, little grows in this cold, bleak landscape. The few people who live in the west are mostly nomadic herdsmen, and farmers who grow barley in sheltered valleys during the short summer.

To the north of the plateau, the high land drops down. Rain seldom reaches this far into the continent, and as a result, a large part of this north-west region is desert. People manage to farm in the scattered oases by using underground irrigation systems.

From the mountains of western China, going east, the land steps down like a giant staircase. Great rivers flow out of the mountains and bring fertile silt to the wide, flat plains further east. These plains are rich farming land.

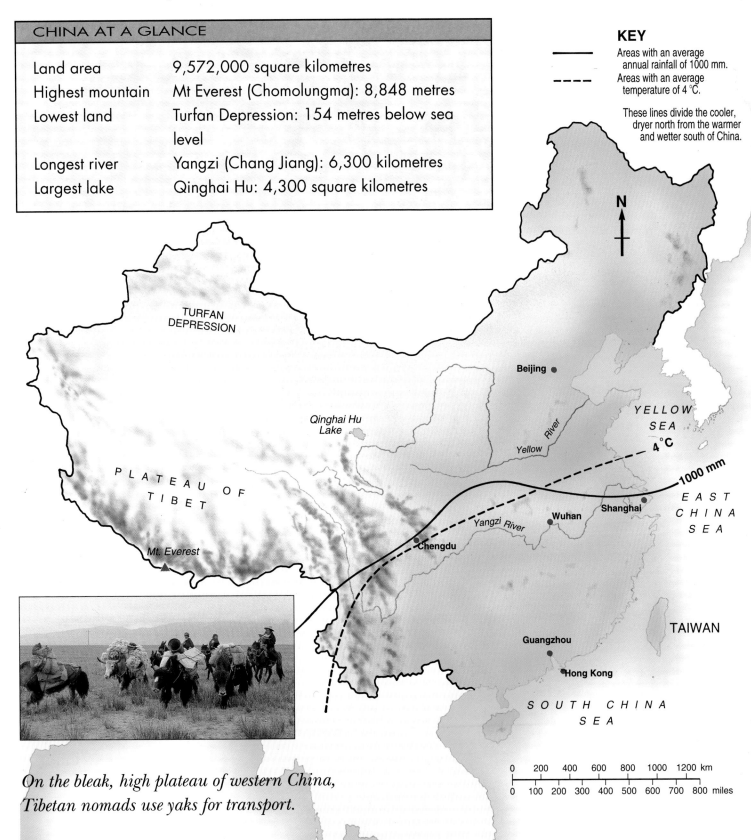

CHINA AT A GLANCE

Land area	9,572,000 square kilometres
Highest mountain	Mt Everest (Chomolungma): 8,848 metres
Lowest land	Turfan Depression: 154 metres below sea level
Longest river	Yangzi (Chang Jiang): 6,300 kilometres
Largest lake	Qinghai Hu: 4,300 square kilometres

KEY

————— Areas with an average annual rainfall of 1000 mm.

- - - - - Areas with an average temperature of 4 °C.

These lines divide the cooler, dryer north from the warmer and wetter south of China.

N

TURFAN DEPRESSION

Qinghai Hu Lake

PLATEAU OF TIBET

Mt. Everest

Beijing

Yellow River

YELLOW SEA

4 °C

1000 mm

EAST CHINA SEA

Yangzi River

Wuhan

Shanghai

Chengdu

TAIWAN

Guangzhou

Hong Kong

SOUTH CHINA SEA

| 0 | 200 | 400 | 600 | 800 | 1000 | 1200 km |
| 0 | 100 | 200 | 300 | 400 | 500 | 600 | 700 | 800 miles |

On the bleak, high plateau of western China, Tibetan nomads use yaks for transport.

The enormous Yellow River is surrounded by the wide, flat North China Plain.

The biggest rivers are the Yangzi River (called the Chang Jiang in Chinese) and the Yellow River (Huang He). Their valleys are home to most of China's huge population. The Yangzi River roughly divides eastern China into two: the warm, rainy south and the cold, dry north.

The Yellow River flows west to east across northern China and has created a massive flood plain known as the North China Plain. This area has always been intensively farmed, but people have to rely on irrigation because the rainfall can be low and unreliable.

The staple crop of the north is wheat, which is used to make noodles. Other grain crops that are grown include sorghum, maize and millet, as well as soya beans and all sorts of fruit and vegetables. Rapeseed and peanuts are used to make oil, and one of the main cash crops in central China is cotton.

'Di shao ren zhong.'
'The land is scarce and the people are many.'
– Old Chinese proverb

FLOODS

Throughout China's long history, terrible floods have devastated the land and people's homes. The worst have been caused by the Yellow and Yangzi rivers. In 1938, almost 1 million people died when the Yellow river burst its banks. During the last 45 years, flood-control works such as building dams, dredging and strengthening banks have tried to prevent further disasters, but during the summer of 1998, the Yangzi river and its tributaries burst through their flood barriers, killing over 4,000 people in one of the worst floods to hit China for 130 years. In 1999, over 800 people died in China's floods.

The Yangzi river valley has fertile land, good water supplies and a moderate climate, making it an important farming area. To the south, the climate gradually becomes hotter and wetter until in the far south it is sub-tropical: warm and wet all year round. In spring, the landscape is like a carpet of fresh green as shoots of rice poke up through water-filled paddy fields, each neatly contained by a low earth bank. Other crops of the south include tea, tobacco, silk, rubber and fruits.

Rice is grown in flooded paddy fields as it needs lots of water. Southern China's climate is warm and wet, providing the ideal conditions.

CLIMATE IN CHINA				
	Beijing	Shanghai	Hong Kong	Lhasa
Average monthly temperature				
Jan	-5°C	3°C	16°C	2°C
July	27°C	27°C	29°C	15°C
Average yearly rainfall (mm)	700	1142	1815	610

Above Fertile land is precious in China. Many people living in this town grow their own vegetables on the plots by the river.

Below Few farmers can afford machinery, and it is difficult to use on small, terraced fields. Water buffalo are often used for ploughing in the south.

Vegetables are grown all over China wherever space can be found. Row after row of neatly planted cabbages, onions and beans tuck in between buildings and roads on the edge of towns and cities. Villages and towns also often have specially built ponds for fish, such as carp.

Despite China's size, only about 10 per cent of the land can be cultivated because of the huge areas of mountain, desert and open steppe. The Chinese have developed all sorts of methods to make the best of the land they have. Hillsides have been terraced for thousands of years. Another method is to use night-soil (human waste) which is put on the fields as fertilizer; the Chinese do not waste useful things. A farming technique practised in many areas is double cropping, where a second crop is planted between the rows of the first.

'With a large population, our country needs to consume vast quantities of food each day. If we pay no attention to agriculture, we'll suffer untold misery. Shikou has developed on the basis of agriculture, and we'll carry on this tradition and do a good job in the fields.'
– Jia Xinwen, aged 48, farmer in Shikou, north China

Due to the lack of machinery, everyone works together to thresh wheat during harvest time on the North China Plain.

AGRICULTURE AND INDUSTRY

Of China's total workforce, 60 per cent work on the land and 17 per cent work in industry. However, agriculture contributes only 26 per cent of China's total wealth, compared with industry's 42 per cent.

Source: *CIA Factbook, 2000*

Most farmers do not have much machinery, and so work the land by hand. Women in poorer regions can be seen slowly hoeing the soil with babies slung on their backs. In the south, water buffalo do heavy work such as ploughing, and in the north, ponies take produce to and from the market.

People and cities

China has twelve cities, each with more than 2 million inhabitants. The population is concentrated in the fertile eastern part of the country.

People of Chinese race are called Han Chinese. From the area around the Yellow River, where China's civilization began nearly 5,000 years ago, the Han people spread outwards, settling lands further and further afield. Over the centuries they took over lands belonging to other races and brought them into the growing Chinese empire.

About 92 per cent of the population are Han Chinese; this leaves nearly 100 million non-Chinese. Whereas the Han Chinese mostly live in the well-farmed and developed east of China, many of the minority people (the non-Chinese) live in the border regions or remoter parts of the country. The west of China, in particular, is home to a large number of the fifty-five different minority groups, such as the Tibetans and the Muslim Uighurs.

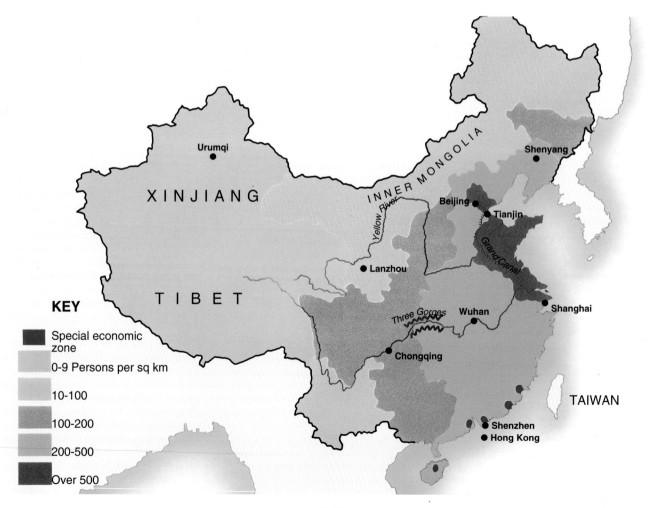

Urumqi

XINJIANG

INNER MONGOLIA

Shenyang

Yellow River

Beijing

Tianjin

Grand Canal

Lanzhou

TIBET

Three Gorges

Wuhan

Shanghai

Chongqing

TAIWAN

Shenzhen

Hong Kong

KEY

- Special economic zone
- 0-9 Persons per sq km
- 10-100
- 100-200
- 200-500
- Over 500

12

Few people in China own a car. Most rely on bicycles for transport.

Most of China's people live in the east of the country because that is the most productive region. The result is that about 90 per cent of the population is squashed into 17 per cent of the whole country's land area. This makes a very crowded landscape; the density of the population in

parts of eastern China is greater than Bangladesh, the most densely populated country in the world. In these areas, virtually no land remains untouched by human hand.

Almost all the big cities have grown up in the east, and they are huge. Over sixty cities have more than one million people. The busy streets are a mass of bicycles in the rush hour as everyone makes their way to and from work. The large number of people means that living space is restricted. Most families have no more than a two-roomed flat. Although some old buildings remain, many have been pulled down so that streets are lined with rows of new, and often ugly, concrete blocks. Towns suffer from bad air pollution. This is worse in winter because everyone uses coal fires that give off fumes and cause smog, a mixture of smoke and fog.

A block of flats in the city of Xian. Living space is limited in the densely populated cities and most families must share only a few small rooms.

13

Large cities lie along the banks of both the Yangzi and the Yellow rivers. The Yangzi serves as a workplace, well and drain to the millions of people who live along its banks. It is one of China's ancient highways, allowing ships to sail east-west across China, from the coast to the interior. Most cities are therefore ports. Shanghai, at the mouth of the Yangzi River, is China's largest city. It is often thought of, by the Chinese, as the centre of fashion and new ideas. This is partly because Shanghai has a history of contact with foreigners who traded and settled in the large port.

Nowadays, Guangzhou and other cities along the south-east coast, particularly those near Hong Kong, are also seen by the Chinese as the trendsetters. All these coastal cities have benefited from their access to the outside world and are important manufacturing centres, producing all sorts of goods for the developing Chinese market.

Beijing became China's capital during the reign of the Mongols, who invaded China from lands to the north about 700 years ago. Even though it is in the far north of China, Beijing remains the capital today. Together with the nearby city of Tianjin, it forms a huge, sprawling urban area.

POPULATION OF CHINA'S MAJOR CITIES	
	millions
Shanghai	9.4
Beijing	7.0
Tianjin	5.8
Shenyang	4.5
Wuhan	3.7

Shanghai is China's largest city and one of its most important ports. Because of its links with the outside world, it is one of the most developed places in China.

Severe pollution of air and water is common in many parts of China.

The far north-east of China is an important coal and steel-producing region. The cities here, such as Shenyang, developed to process iron, coal and steel, and also have hundreds of industries producing heavy machinery. Out-of-date, gloomy factories billow smoke into the air. The cloud of pollution hanging over Benxi, near Shenyang, is famous for being one of two artificial things, said to be seen from outer space by astronauts. The other is the famous, and far more beautiful, Great Wall of China.

SPECIAL ECONOMIC ZONES

SEZs were created under the new 'open door' policy of the late 1970s. They were cities or areas on the coast where, for the first time under the communist government, Chinese companies could experiment with private ownership, and foreign businesses were encouraged to set up. It was hoped that the Chinese would learn from the up-to-date technology brought in by outsiders, as well as reap some of the profits of the new enterprises. Business has boomed in the SEZs.

Resources and transport

Unlike many countries, China is rich in resources such as coal, oil and minerals. However, despite this, China is rather like a crippled giant. Its old-fashioned production methods, and its hopelessly crowded transport network, make it difficult to supply the endless needs of its fast-growing population and industries.

POWER

The main source of power in China is coal, both for industry and for homes in the cities. Despite the pollution it causes, coal is the cheapest and easiest form of fuel for most Chinese people to use. Although China has the largest coal reserves in the world, they are not mined or used efficiently because of outdated machinery. Most of the coal is found in the north. It is not easy to transport to other parts of the country because it is so bulky. Many places face serious power shortages. Shanghai, for example, seldom has more than a few days' supply and the city often has power cuts.

ENERGY USED IN INDUSTRY

China uses an average of 1.64 tonnes of coal to make one tonne of steel, whereas it takes 0.7 tonnes in India and only 0.3 tonnes in Japan.

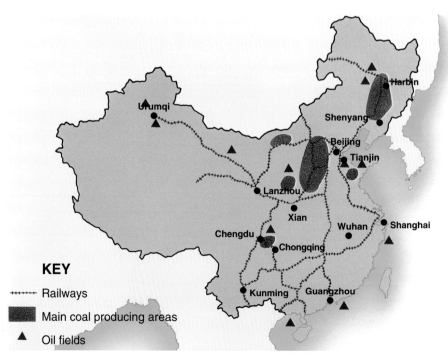

KEY

++++++ Railways

◼ Main coal producing areas

▲ Oil fields

Major cities, coal and oil fields are linked by a network of railways.

16

'My family of eight used to cut firewood in the mountains for cooking. About ten days out of every month went into this activity. Now the fifty or so families in our village use electricity to cook meals and heat water, and because of that we save several hundred thousand kilos of timber and 4,000 working days a month.'
— **Wang Defu, peasant in north Sichuan**

Fuel, even for cooking food, can be scarce. People use small stoves to make the most efficient use of the fuel they have.

Oil is becoming more important as a fuel in China. However, much of the oil is in distant, unpopulated areas, such as the deserts of the north-west, and it has to be taken through pipelines to where it is needed.

Hydroelectricity is another growing source of energy in China. Hundreds of dams have been built, taking advantage of the country's many rivers. Some small schemes produce enough electricity for a village; others, on rivers such as the Yellow River supply huge networks of power. Like other sources of energy in China, however, a lot of the hydroelectricity is produced in remote regions, and not where it is most wanted.

ENERGY USE

The amount of energy that a Chinese person uses in a year is less than a typical American family uses in their car in three weeks.

Much of rural China still depends on plants to provide fuel. Every year, millions of peasants search desperately for enough fuel to cook their simple meals. They burn plant stalks and straw, but also turn to the countryside, stripping hillsides of trees and bushes. This has severe effects on the environment, such as erosion and desertification.

Electricity can be produced by using the power of falling water. The Yellow River has been dammed in several places to provide power for industry.

17

Main roads, like this one in the mountains of western China, are often washed away by sudden rain storms.

TRANSPORT

As well as shortages of energy, another important problem in China is a lack of transport. Trains are the most usual long-distance transport, because few people have cars and the roads are very poor. Although China has thousands of kilometres of railways, they are not enough. Trains are always packed with people, and goods trains, some of which still run on steam, can be delayed for hours.

During 1992, coal processors in northern China and Inner Mongolia had to stop production because they could not find enough transport to take the coal to its consumers. Many users of the coal were in coastal cities, such as Shanghai, and manufacturers there had to stop work because they had no power. The government is planning to build electric lines along important supply routes and more rail tracks to improve the situation.

New roads are being constructed in some areas, but in some parts of China, even main roads are dirt tracks. So much of the country is mountainous that it is a struggle to keep roads in good repair, especially when there are frequent landslides.

Boats have always been used for transport, but the big rivers are mostly in the south and the eastern plains, where the rainfall is regular enough to keep the rivers full, and the land is flat enough for canals to be built.

18

'Mr Sun, who had invited guests for dinner, rushed home to prepare the meal. He turned on the tap – not a drop of water came out. The large thermos [vacuum flask] in which he kept his drinking water was empty as well. He ran downstairs to the corner shop – too late, they were all out of mineral water. He had no choice but to buy several bottles of beer and cook with that.'
– **China Today**, *April 1994*

Even in large cities, some people still get all their water from wells.

WATER SHORTAGES

In the early 1950s, water for the city of Beijing was drawn up in wells from 5 metres below the surface of the ground; now it is necessary to drill down 50 metres to find water. Other parts of the north are also desperate for water. Even the mighty Yellow River runs dry at certain times of the year because of the vast quantities of water drawn out of it.

About four-fifths of China's water use is for irrigation. The rest is needed by industries and households. It is believed that over 300 of China's cities face serious shortages.

To try and solve the problem in the north, it has been decided to divert water from the Yangzi River, which has a much greater and more regular flow of water than rivers in the north. The Grand Canal, built many hundreds of years ago to link Beijing with the Yangzi basin, will be the main water channel. So far, no account seems to have been taken of what the effect might be on the Yangzi River.

At certain times of the year, the great Yellow River runs dry because so much water is drawn off for irrigation.

19

THE THREE GORGES PROJECT

About half-way along its course, the mighty Yangzi River passes through mountains. The river has carved deep gorges out of the rock. These gorges are famous for their scenic beauty, and thousands of tourists visit them every year. However, work has begun on the world's biggest dams there. The scheme is known as the Three Gorges Project. Work began in 1993 and is scheduled for completion in 2009.

Engineers see the project as vital to control flooding downstream and to harness the great river's power for hydroelectricity. They say it will supply energy to the growing cities along the Yangzi valley and even cities on the coast. Planners believe that life for all the 350 million people who live within the Yangzi basin will be improved.

Others are more critical of the project. They point out that the dam will ruin the beauty of the gorges, which has been praised in Chinese literature for hundreds of years. At least ten towns and many villages will be drowned by the reservoir, which will be over 340 kilometres long. More than a million people will lose their homes and new cities are already being built for them. The dam will bring serious environmental changes, affecting wildlife and possibly even the climate of area. These results have been seen in other large dam projects all over the world. If the dam collapses in the future, it will be catastrophic for the millions of people living downstream.

'. . . I can only tell you that the local people want us to build the dam. Yes, there'll be an environmental problem and we'll have to relocate a million people – half of them city dwellers and the other half villagers.'
– Zhang Guangdou, chief engineer, Three Gorges Project

Background to developing China

For several decades, before the Communist Party took power in 1949, China was split into areas controlled by warlords. A weak, central government controlled part of the country. The rural peasants, who made up most of the population, suffered at the hands of rich landlords and because of constant fighting. The chaos made natural disasters, such as droughts and floods, much worse.

The Communists finally won power in a civil war. Land was given to the peasants to work collectively. Large public works were begun, such as flood control along the Yellow River. New factories, schools and hospitals were built, often by communes (groups of people working together). For most people, the standard of living improved dramatically.

However, Communist rule has had its troubles. Political turmoil and bad economic decisions brought hardship to many, and set back progress. By shutting itself off from the rest of world, China never gained from trade or exchange of technology.

People's lives were totally controlled by the government. They were told what to grow, where to live, where to work, what to do in their spare time and what books they could read. Nearly everyone belonged to a commune or work unit that provided housing, schools, health care and leisure facilities.

Mao Zedong, China's great communist leader from 1949 to 1976. His policies improved the standard of living for many, but brought misery to others.

In the 1980s, reforms were begun that are now taking China on a new course. From what was a centralized, controlled economy, where the government made all the decisions, the country has begun moving to a market economy, where people decide for themselves what to buy and sell.

The Chinese started to run their own businesses, from bicycle-repair shops, vegetable and clothing stalls, to manufacturing workshops. Farmers were allowed to grow what they liked and to sell it where they wanted.

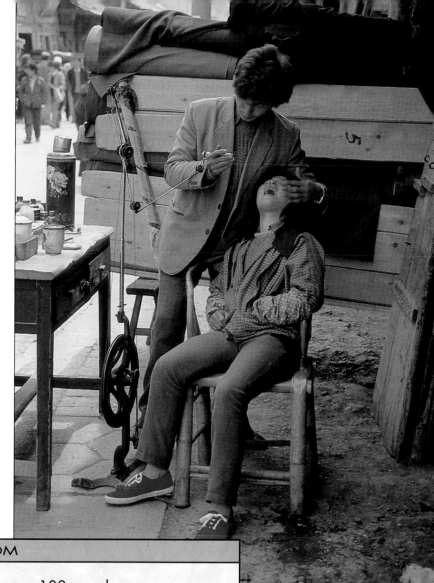

CHINA'S CONSUMER BOOM

Number of household appliances per 100 people

	1985	1989	1992
Bicycles	21.1	32.4	38.5
Cameras	1.1	1.8	2.3
Refrigerators	0.4	2.3	3.4
Televisions	6.6	14.7	19.5
Washing machines	2.9	7.7	10.0
Sewing machines	9.3	12.0	12.8

China Statistical Yearbook, 1993

Source: *World Bank Development Report*, 1993

Above A street dentist treats one of his patients. Running a private business in China today can take almost any form.

Right Modern mountain bikes are very popular in China – for those who can afford them.

Above In the last fifteen years or so, more people have been able to buy luxury items such as cameras and televisions. This chart shows how the number of luxuries has risen since 1985.

MEASURING DEVELOPMENT

One way to measure the development of a country is to work out how much wealth it produces. A country's Gross Domestic Product (GDP) is the total value of all the goods and services it produces in a year.

A recent World Bank report referred to China as an 'economic superpower' because its total GDP ranked second in the world after the USA. However, China's GDP is high because it has so many workers. If you divide the total wealth by the number of workers in China, the amount each person produces is low.

Many people are making money and incomes are rising. Until now, few Chinese would have been able to afford (or even find in the shops) luxuries such as watches, radios, refrigerators or televisions.

'Breaking the iron rice bowl'

Wang Hua and his wife live in the city of Lanzhou, which lies in northern China on the Yellow River.

Mr Wang has the sort of job that used to be the dream of every young Chinese person. It is a 'safe' job, in a company owned by the government that produces fertilizers. Mr Wang's wage is low but the company gives him a flat to live in, his daughter goes to the company's school, the family can use sports facilities and a hospital, and they expect to be looked after when Mr Wang retires. Secure jobs like this used to be known by the Chinese as an 'iron rice bowl', because they guaranteed a reasonable standard of living.

Mr Wang's company used to sell all its fertilizers to the government – a reliable market. However, because of the new changes in China, the company now has to find its own customers and compete with other producers around the country. The factory uses old machinery,

A chemical factory in Lanzhou provides jobs and support for many people, but also causes bad pollution.

Old-fashioned machinery and unsafe working conditions are problems for many of China's industries.

has more workers than it needs, and managers like Mr Wang have no experience in controlling a tight budget and selling the fertilizers.

Like two-thirds of China's state industries, the factory is losing money. Mr Wang and the other managers are struggling to keep the factory going.

One of the problems is that the factory does not just support Mr Wang. It also looks after his wife and daughter, and his elderly mother who lives with the family. Although the company employs about 3,000 people directly, it has to care for about 17,000 people who are the dependants of its workers. Every year, about one-third of its budget goes to paying pensions and providing benefits for all these people.

The factory is a maze of ancient pipework, hardly updated since it was built, and the old-fashioned machinery is dangerous and pumps out evil-smelling fumes into the air of Lanzhou. New equipment is needed, but costs have to be cut if the company is to make goods to sell at competitive prices.

One way the company is surviving is in sidelines. Last year it set up a taxi company and a clothing shop, both of which are successful money-makers. They employ factory workers who would otherwise have little else to do. Even so, the company is having to cut down on the benefits that workers receive, and is even making workers redundant.

Unemployment is facing people all over China, and for the first time in his life, Mr Wang's future looks uncertain. Slowly, the iron rice bowl is beginning to crack.

Many schools have almost no money, so there are hardly any books or equipment.

EDUCATION

The Chinese people believe education is important, but schools are hopelessly underfunded, overcrowded and ill-equipped because of the lack of government money. Many schools have to run sideline businesses to keep going.

Compared to other large, poor nations, China has an average standard of primary education, but it is far behind in ensuring its people receive higher education.

STANDARDS OF EDUCATION

Even though 80 per cent of Chinese people are now able to read and write:

- 38 per cent of adult women are illiterate.
- 68 per cent of people living in Tibet cannot read or write.
- One-third of children living in the country are unlikely to complete their education.
- Only 2 per cent of people aged 20–24 are in higher education (compared with double that in India and Pakistan).
- Universities and colleges only have places for 830,000, although 2.8 million will take entry exams.

Because many people cannot read or write, they pay professional letter-writers to help them with important or difficult letters.

Changing workplace

A few years ago, because all work and housing was controlled by the government, Chinese people needed permission to change jobs or move to another area. As a result, people had little choice in the type of work they could do or where it would be. With the new freedoms, many Chinese people are on the move, looking for different and better-paid jobs.

RURAL/URBAN DIFFERENCES

Average annual incomes (yuan)

	1978	1985	1989	1992
Rural	134	398	602	784
Urban	316	685	1261	1826

There are still about 100 million people below the poverty line (considered to be 200 yuan). About 30 million of these do not have enough to eat. Most of them live in rural areas.

Millions of people are travelling to where they hear there are good opportunities, usually the large cities. Some go no further than their nearest city. However, most are going to Beijing, Tianjin and the coastal towns and cities such as Shanghai, Guangzhou and the Special Economic Zones, where the economy is growing fastest. On some days, more than 500,000 migrants were pouring through Shanghai station. They have swelled the city's population by 2.5 million.

People have migrated from rural areas to the more affluent cities nearer the coast.

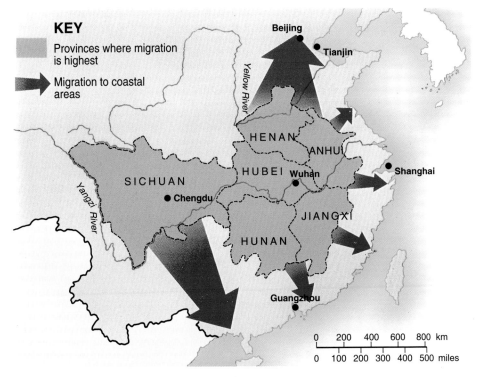

KEY

Provinces where migration is highest

Migration to coastal areas

Beijing · Tianjin

Yellow River

HENAN · ANHUI

HUBEI · Wuhan · Shanghai

SICHUAN · Chengdu

Yangzi River

JIANGXI

HUNAN

Guangzhou

| 0 | 200 | 400 | 600 | 800 km |
| 0 | 100 | 200 | 300 | 400 | 500 miles |

Many migrants fail to find a job, and return home after camping out on the streets for a few days. Among them are farmers from poorer inland areas seeking work in construction, or in factories. Those who get work often earn three times what they could in the countryside.

'Going down to the sea'

'Going down to the sea' (*xiahai* in Chinese) is used to describe leaving government-run organizations or businesses and trying private enterprise. Xie Zulian used to be a middle-school teacher earning 200 yuan a month, but he took the risk, left his job and set up on his own as a tourist guide. Now he earns 800 yuan a month.

He speaks good English and lives in an area of southern China famed for the beauty of its scenery. Thousands of foreign tourists come to see it every year. Zulian offers trips to see local sights, and organizes travel tickets for foreigners who cannot speak Chinese. This business is quite risky because it depends on the tourist trade, but Zulian finds it much more interesting and exciting than being a teacher.

He has not only given up a secure job, but also the free, two-roomed flat owned by the school, and the pension he would have had when he retired. He is now renting a tiny

People like Xie Zulian help foreigners to travel in China. Some go on bicycle tours to see what life in China is really like.

28

A family has lunch in the main room of their flat. Many companies give their workers somewhere to live at a very low rent.

room for himself and his wife, but he plans to try and buy his own flat in the future, if he can make enough money.

A friend of Zulian, Huang Gujian, has decided not to 'go down to the sea' but to keep his safe job in the local bottle factory. Gujian's wife, however, has gone into private enterprise with a hairdressing business. The young Chinese are now very fashion-conscious and she is doing a roaring trade. This way the Huangs get the best of both worlds: the benefits that go with Huang Gujian's work as well as the chance of making good money through his wife's business.

'. . .*if you* xiahai, *you lose something. The main thing is housing. Private companies are building housing, but it's very expensive. It's a big problem. I have another friend who really wants to [xiahai], but he can't because he will lose his free accommodation. He has a two-bedroom flat: a great achievement in China.'*
– Xie Zulian, self-employed tourist guide, South China

Young women, such as these in Shenzhen, enjoy the latest fashions.

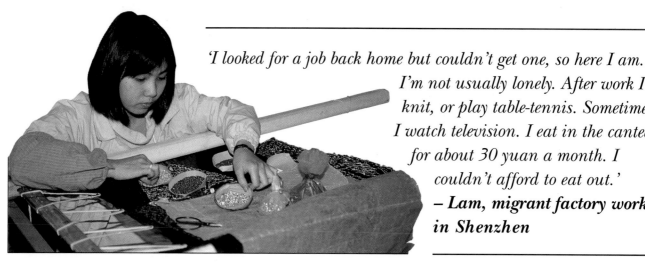

'I looked for a job back home but couldn't get one, so here I am. I'm not usually lonely. After work I knit, or play table-tennis. Sometimes I watch television. I eat in the canteen for about 30 yuan a month. I couldn't afford to eat out.'
– Lam, migrant factory worker in Shenzhen

Migrant workers come to the cities in search of jobs and better wages than those they can earn at home.

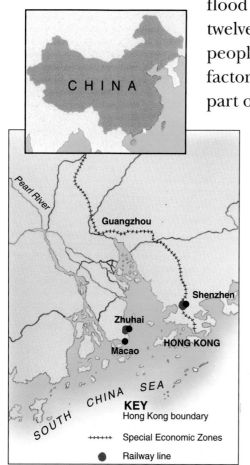

SHENZHEN

Shenzhen is one of China's Special Economic Zones (SEZs). It is located in the far south, near Hong Kong, which was a British Colony until 1997. Because it is so close to Hong Kong, Shenzen has been the most successful SEZ in attracting foreign business.

Shenzhen has become like a gold-rush town; people flood in from all over China. From a village of 10,000 just twelve years ago, it has grown into a city of about 2.5 million people, with modern high-rise buildings, nightclubs and factories that sprawl out into the countryside. Shenzhen is part of a fast-developing region: between here and the city of Guangzhou, two hours away by train, there is now an almost continuous scar where paddy fields have been bulldozed ready for further building.

Lam, aged 23, came to Shenzhen ten months ago from the north-east where she could not find work. Permits are required to work in Shenzhen because of its special status, but Lam just paid a bribe and stayed on.

She found work in a factory, earning what for her was good money, and she sends most of her wage home to her family. The hours are long, she lives in a dormitory with eight other girls, and she is only able to go home once a year. However, she is single and young, like most people who have come to Shenzhen, so she thinks it is better than staying at home.

Development in the countryside

Even though cities are growing, most people in China still live in the countryside. Away from the large urban areas and coastal regions, remote parts of the country are very backward. Peasants here get some benefit from the improving economy, but most suffer because the cost of everything has gone up due to inflation.

One new source of income, which has helped rural areas since the early 1980s, is the thousands of small businesses set up, either by villagers working together or privately. Village and small township businesses now make up about half of China's rural output. They employ about 100 million people.

Below Villagers work together on a project to build new terraced fields for their crops.

Above *New businesses in China can be large or small. Here, an enterprising man has set up his own small stall to sell rat poison.*

A large part of northern China is covered in this pale 'yellow earth'. Because there is little plant or tree cover, the soil is easily washed away by rain, and erosion is very common.

YELLOW EARTH

Shikou is a village in north China. It lies in a hilly region of fine, pale, yellow soil, which is fertile and easy to work. Wheat, beans, fruit and tobacco are grown on the terraced hillsides.

Despite the crops that can be grown, the area has problems, and remains poor and underdeveloped. Often, there are droughts and then sudden storms that quickly erode the fragile soil. Fields and roads are swept away and deep gullies are left. This erosion has been made worse because the region has been almost completely deforested.

Many of the houses are cut, like caves, into the hillsides. Inside, as well as ordinary furniture, there is a wide, raised brick platform called a *kang*, which is heated from underneath. In the bitter winters, to keep warm enough, everyone sleeps together on the *kang*. On plots of land nearby, villagers grow maize, and a few chickens usually scratch around in the dusty courtyard outside the houses. Life is better than it was a few years ago: people can now occasionally afford to add a little meat to their daily bowl of noodles and vegetables, but they still work hard just to earn a basic living.

Many of the houses in this region are cut, like caves, into the soft earth. This helps to keep people warm during the freezing winters.

32

Tractor drivers cross the Yellow River by ferry. They earn money by taking goods and people to and from market.

Jia Xinwen lives in Shikou with his wife, son, daughter-in-law and grandson. Mr Jia is part of the orchard team, a group of village farmers who grow peaches. The group has a contract with the village, which owns the land. The group gives some of its profit to the village every year and then splits the remainder among its members. One villager bought a tractor, and set up business transporting goods to the nearest town. He has done quite well, and with his profits was the first person in the village to buy his own television.

Recently, a reservoir was built nearby. It has made watering the fields much easier and has brought drinking-water by tap to Shikou. Some villages still depend on well-water for all their needs. However, Mr Jia is worried that local people and officials are concerned with making money for themselves, and are not thinking about the long-term needs of the area. For example, irrigation channels are falling into disrepair and the government is not building new roads that the area desperately needs.

'Everyone's been buying radios in the last few years. They cost a fortune: 100 kilos of persimmons [a fruit] each. Of course, if we had a government road they'd be much cheaper.'
– Jia Xinwen, aged 48, farmer in Shikou

PEARL RIVER DELTA

In the far south of China, as the Pearl River nears the sea, it spreads out into a fertile, flat delta. Nearby are the large urban areas of Guangzhou and Hong Kong. As well as growing vegetables to supply the huge city populations, farmers of the delta raise silkworms.

Along the edges of fish-ponds, mulberry trees grow. The leaves are collected every day and fed to the silkworms. When they have grown to their full size, the silkworms make fine threads which they form into cocoons. These threads are made into silk cloth. The silkworm droppings are fed to the fish and the fertile mud from the bottom of the ponds is used to fertilize the mulberry trees.

Above Silkworms spin silk filaments to make their cocoons. The strong threads are unravelled, dyed and woven to make cloth.

TREE PLANTING

As huge areas of China have been stripped of trees, the government has been carrying out a mass reafforestation programme. It is claimed that since 1949, the area of forested land has gone up from between 5 and 8 per cent to nearly 13 per cent. During a campaign in the early 1980s, millions of people were told to help plant trees. Although millions of trees were planted, only about one-fifth of them have survived, as the trees have not been watered or looked after. There is still a serious shortage of timber, and the harmful environmental effects of losing trees, such as soil erosion and disappearing wildlife, are being felt all over the country.

Known as the 'Great Green Wall', a long belt of trees has been planted across parts of northern China. It helps to stabilize the soil and prevent the loose desert sand from spreading.

34

Silk farmers

Li Jincai was a local farmer who began by raising silkworms. He then borrowed money from a bank and opened his own factory to manufacture silk cloth. He was so successful that he sells his cloth all over China. Li's family no longer have to work on the land. Now they supervise people who work for them. His wife, however, still bicycles off to work in a local clothing factory every day, just to keep a safe job.

'In the 1960s and 1970s, when the bell rang, everybody went to the same field, did the same work and got the same pay. Now it's quite different. As long as you're not lazy, you can become well-to-do.'
– Li Jincai, silk producer,
Pearl River Delta

The Jincais have built a new, brick house decorated with coloured tiles, and they have a Japanese television, much more expensive and better quality than a Chinese-made one. They are able to afford to send their son to a private school in a nearby town; they believe he will get a better education there than in the poorer state school.

Some villages in the delta have found they could make money by just building and renting out factory space to new industries, so large areas of farmland have been built on. This 'easy money' has altered some villagers' outlook on life. They now consider farm work beneath them, and leave the hard labour to the immigrants from poorer parts of China, who come to the region seeking jobs.

Silk cloth has been made in China for thousands of years. It is used for beautiful clothes, sold to tourists and exported to countries all over the world.

Boundaries and empire

The economic development of China's border regions depends as much on people's race and ownership of territory as on economics itself.

Some of the minority people, such as the Tibetans, Mongolians and Muslims, whose land has been under Chinese rule for many years, are calling for independence. So far, the Chinese government has firmly put down any sign of unrest. However, if whole provinces, such as Tibet, decide to revolt, it would not be an easy task to hold together an empire the size of China.

At the other end of the country, China is adding to its empire. In 1997, the British colony of Hong Kong was returned to mainland China.

Off the east coast of the mainland there is also the wealthy island of Taiwan, whose independent government refuses to accept Communist China at present. Even so, Taiwan may one day become part of China again. These two territories are important to China because the people are Chinese, well-educated and could bring modern technology and much-needed investment to mainland China.

Tibetan monks, watched by local people and Chinese police, parade at a festival.

Muslims at prayer in north-west China. In recent years they have been allowed more religious freedom by the Chinese.

THE MUSLIMS OF XINJIANG

In 1993 and again in 1997, Muslims in north-west China rioted and many were arrested. These were not the first times there has been trouble in the huge border province of Xinjiang, remote from China's heartland in the east.

The Silk Road, a trading route since ancient times, passes through Xinjiang's deserts and oases. It has long been important to the largely Muslim population of the region.

The remote regions of Xinjiang and Tibet are influenced by the nearby countries of Kazakhstan, Russia, Mongolia, India and Pakistan.

These Muslims belong to two main groups: the Uighurs and the Kazakhs, both of whom have more in common with their Central-Asian neighbours to the west than with the Chinese.

When it came to power, the communist Chinese government persecuted Muslims as well as other religious groups in China. Mosques were razed to the ground and protesting Muslims jailed. Everyone had to learn Chinese. Settlers were brought into Xinjiang from eastern China, diluting the Muslim population. The city of Urumqi, for example, is now 80 per cent Chinese. The Chinese brought few benefits to the local people and development is slower than in the rest of the country.

37

Within the last few years, China's western borders have been opened for the first time since the beginning of communist rule. Russians, Kazakhs and other Central-Asian people have been flooding in to trade. Opening the borders is also letting in ideas: the Kazakhs of China can now see their fellow Muslims running their own country, Kazakhstan.

Despite more religious freedom in recent years, and the use again of Arabic script in schools, some Muslims would like to be free of Chinese control. However, the Chinese are unlikely to give up Xinjiang province easily. Rich oil deposits have been discovered there, and there may also be valuable mineral deposits in the province's desert areas.

Some Kazakh people are still nomads. They live in tents, called yurts, which they move when they take their animals to fresh pasture.

'If people fight the Chinese, I like that. If I die in that fight, I'm very happy, because Xinjiang is Turkestan, not China.'
– 24-year-old Muslim in Xinjiang
Herald Tribune, 16 October 1990

38

The Potala Palace in Lhasa was once the home of Tibet's religious leader, the Dalai Lama. He fled when the Chinese took over and now lives in exile abroad. The Chinese have opened the palace as a tourist attraction.

TIBETANS

Tibet has only been part of China since the 1950s. It is a mountainous land. Traditionally, many Tibetans are nomadic, herding yaks and living in tents. They follow the Buddhist religion. When the Chinese took, control of Tibet, they destroyed thousands of religious buildings and imprisoned any Tibetans who resisted. Chinese people settled in Tibet's capital city, Lhasa, and old Tibetan buildings were torn down to make way for new concrete blocks. Now the Chinese are rebuilding temples, mainly so they can make money out of rich Western tourists who want to visit Tibet. Many Tibetans would like to be rid of the Chinese for good.

The colourful festivals and costumes of the Tibetan people attract many Western tourists to the region.

Hong Kong was once a fishing village, but is now one of the richest cities in the world.

In 1989, many Tibetans rose up against Chinese rule. The Chinese army was sent in to put down the revolt. That same year, Chinese students demonstrated in Tianenmen Square in Beijing to express their wish for democracy. The government sent in soldiers and tanks to stop the demonstration and hundreds of people were killed. In both events, China used force to prevent objections to its rule.

HONG KONG

In 1842, when the British acquired Hong Kong, it was an uninhabited island on the south coast of China. Since then, it has developed into one of the world's greatest trading and financial centres. The average GDP per person in Hong Kong is far higher than in mainland China.

In 1997, the British left and Hong Kong reverted to China. Before the handover, many of Hong Kong's people were fearful about becoming part of China, even though most were Chinese. The Chinese government reassured them that Hong Kong could keep its economic system, with the slogan 'One Country, Two Systems'.

The handover went smoothly. Hong Kong still has a separate economy and manages most of its own affairs.

The territory of Hong Kong, although very small, has become one of the wealthiest places in the world.

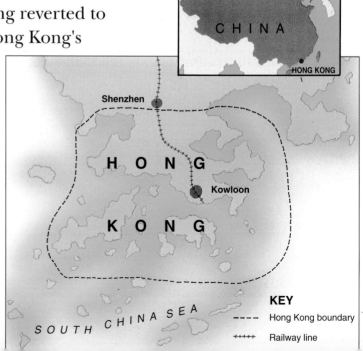

China's future

The size of China's population is the main factor influencing the country's development. When the Communists came to power in 1949, the civil war ended and health and living standards improved. This gave rise to a population explosion. Nothing was done about curbing the incredible rate at which the population was growing until 1980. Then, a new policy was introduced allowing Chinese couples to have only one child.

Single-child families are now common in China.

POPULATION GROWTH 1949–2000	
1955	615,000,000
1960	662,000,000
1965	725,000,000
1970	830,000,000
1975	924,000,000
1980	987,000,000
1985	1,058,000,000
1990	1,143,000,000
1992	1,171,000,000
1998	1,255,698,000
2000	1,277,588,000
Source: United Nations Population Division	

If a couple had one child they were paid a bonus by the government, but if they had more than one child, they were fined. In cities, a second child would not be given free medical care or schooling. It is amazing that this policy has worked at all in a country where the tradition is to have as many children as possible. The result has been to keep the population growth rate down, way below that of most developing countries.

41

Even with strict birth control, there are still millions of Chinese children needing food, housing and education.

In rural areas, however, there was opposition to the one-child policy because children were needed to help work the land. So in the countryside an exception has been made, allowing families to have two children. Many people are also worried about the single children becoming very spoilt: the Chinese nickname them 'little emperors'.

The Chinese word for population is *renkou*, which means people-mouths. Despite the low population growth rate, there are still about 20 million Chinese born every year, more than the whole population of Australia. They will need more food, more homes, more power; in fact, more of everything. It is a fine balance as to whether there will be enough to go round, even without trying to improve everyone's standard of living.

'If the population continues to grow, there will not be enough grain to feed the people. People will expand on to mountain slopes to obtain more land for cultivation, which can cause soil erosion and the loss of fertilizer. The result will be extensive cultivation but poor harvests. The more land they cultivate, the poorer they become; the poorer they become, the more land they cultivate and the more children they bear; the more children they bear, the poorer they become. This is a vicious cycle.'
– Zhang Zhiliang, Gansu Population Research Centre

Future development in China also depends on politics. Many people believe the new reforms are good, but others would like to return to the old Communist ways with central control of the economy. In the 1980s and early 1990s, Communist leader Deng Xiaoping steered the country towards a more Western-style economy. New leaders continued on the same path when Deng died in 1997.

Unrest may also upset China's development. Stories fill the newspapers of corrupt government officials enjoying lavish entertainment, using public money for their own business deals, and charging illegal taxes. People are losing patience with government officials because of this corruption. There have been demonstrations, and even riots, in protest.

Cyclists in the city of Shenzhen pass a poster showing Deng Xiaoping, China's most important leader during the 1980s and early 1990s.

43

Fur hats for sale in western China. The loss of natural habitats and hunting have brought many wild animals close to extinction.

'Before the 1950s, rich and beautiful forests covered these hills. But after liberation these were cut down to plant rubber trees, build houses and plant crops. The forests used to be full of wild animals . . . wild boar, deer . . . There used to be so many wild animals that you could catch them easily.'
– Huang Hongrui, villager on Hainan Island, south China

Zhangjiajie, one of China's most beautiful national parks.

DEVELOPMENT AND THE ENVIRONMENT

In its fast drive for modernization, China is paying little attention to its environment. In the countryside, large areas of land are suffering from erosion, deforestation and desertification. In towns and cities, the rivers are thick, oily soups of chemicals and sewage, and the air is becoming unsafe to breathe. In Chongqing, an industrial city on the Yangzi River, local coal produces high levels of sulphur. The sulphur is not blown away because the city is surrounded by hills and sheltered from winds. Recently, lamp-posts and buses had to be replaced because they had been eaten away by the acid contained in the rain.

Compared with other developing countries, China has made many advances over the past few decades, such as in providing food, health care and education. However, the majority of the people are still poor and live in crowded conditions with very basic facilities. The present economic boom is bringing wealth to some. It is also adding impossible pressures to China's already stretched resources, and could lead to economic collapse.

Since the new reforms were introduced, most Chinese people are optimistic about their future. As they say: 'The ice has been broken and the path has been opened.'

INDICATORS OF DEVELOPMENT

Development is not just measured in how much people produce. China may have a low GDP per person, but there have been great improvements in health and welfare over the past few decades:

- Infant mortality: 47 deaths per 1,000 births; decreased from 140 in 1960.
- Life expectancy: 70 years; increased from about 40 years in 1950.
- Education: 80 per cent of the population can read and write; up from 20 per cent in 1950.
- Food intake per person: China is almost equal with Japan, one of the richest nations in the world.
- Percentage of population with access to safe water: 72 per cent; in most African countries it is below 50 per cent.

Sources: *The State of the World's Children*, (UNICEF, 2000)

The owner of a small restaurant in central China sees life for her and her family getting better under the new freedoms in China.

'The Chinese are by no means stupid. The backwardness of our economy is simply due to the stranglehold old ideas still have on us. Once we loosen the stranglehold, there'll be no stopping us.'
Cheng Kejie, governor of Guangxi Province

China Today, April 1994

45

Glossary

Altitude The height of the land above sea level.

Buddhist Belonging to Buddhism, the religion founded by a holy man called Buddha, in India in about 500 BC.

Central Asian Coming from countries between China and the Caspian Sea.

Communist A follower of the political idea that everything should be owned and controlled by the community and shared between the people.

Deforested Having removed all the trees from land that was once covered by forest.

Democracy A government system that is elected or chosen by the majority of the people.

Dependants People who rely on others for support.

Desertification The change of fertile land to desert.

Erosion Wearing away of land and soil by the action of water and wind.

Gross Domestic Product (GDP) The total value of all the goods and services produced by a country in a year.

Hydroelectricity Electricity produced by the power of falling water.

Illiterate Not educated, and unable to read.

Inflation A general increase of prices and fall in the value of money.

Irrigation Bringing extra water to help crops grow.

Isolated Being like an island, without influence from outside.

Labour intensive Using many people to work on one thing.

Life expectancy The average age someone can expect to live.

Migrants People who have moved from one town or country to another.

Millet A kind of grain grown as a crop for food.

Muslim Follower of Islam, the religion founded by the Prophet Muhammad.

Nomadic People who do not stay in one place, but move around, often in search of grazing for their animals.

Noodles A food made from wheat flour, rather like spaghetti.

Oases Fertile places in the middle of deserts, where water is usually found.

Peasants People who work on the land, and who are usually quite poor.

Persecution Causing suffering to people, especially because of their religious or political beliefs.

Private enterprise When individuals run their own company or business.

Reafforestation Replanting trees.

Redundant No longer needed, and so dismissed from work.

Self-sufficient Able to look after oneself without help.

Steppe Level, grassy plain, with no trees.

War-lords Commanders of soldiers.

Yak A kind of ox with a thick coat that keeps it warm in freezing weather; yaks survive well at high altitudes.

Yuan The unit of money in China.

Further information

Department for International Development
94 Victoria St, London SW1E 5JL
Website: www.dfid.gov.uk
General information on developing countries.

The Great Britain-China Centre
15 Belgrave Square, London SW1X 8PS
Tel: 020 7235 6696
A good library with information about all aspects of China as well as slides, tapes and videos.

China Now
109 Promenade, Cheltenham, Gloucester GL50 1NW
A magazine produced by the Society for Anglo-Chinese Understanding. Has articles and information about life in China today.

The Cultural Section, Chinese Embassy
49-51 Portland Place, London W1N
Tel: 020 7636 0380
Website: www.chinese-embassy.org.uk

UNICEF
55 Lincoln's Inn Fields, London WC2A 3NB.
Website: www.unicef.org.uk
Resources for schools about people in other lands.

Books to read

Chinese Festivals Cookbook by Stuart Thomson (Hodder Wayland, 2000)
Country Fact Files: China by Catherine Charley (Hodder Wayland, 1994)
A Flavour of China by Julia Waterlow (Hodder Wayland, 1998)
Real World: China by Julia Waterlow (Franklin Watts, 1994)

Films

The Blue Kite: The story of a young boy in Beijing.
The Last Emperor: A historical saga about China's last emperor, who began life a ruler of a huge population, and ended as a gardener. Available on video.
The Story of Qiu Ju: About the life of a peasant woman in rural China.
Yellow Earth: A soldier visits a backward village in 1939, bringing new ideas and hopes to the people who live there.

Index

Numbers in **bold** refer to illustrations.